Still Rocking My Crown

"People can be so pretty but can be so mean at the same time, and at that point their beauty doesn't matter. Who you are on the inside matters the most."

-*Brielle*

Still Rocking My Crown

A memoir about a mother & daughter's experience with alopecia

Written by Brielle Belay and Jenise Belay

Contributions by P. Angel Marie Rogers & Askia Fountain

Published by

Dedication

I would like to dedicate this book to any mother out there who is feeling unsupported, unheard or frustrated when it comes to fighting for their child's health, self-esteem, and well-being. Don't give up!

-Jenise

I want to dedicate this book to anyone who is dealing with hair loss. I want you to know that things will get better. And that your life will be just as full. Keep going!

-Brielle

Foreword

As I sat down to read Jenise and her daughter Brielle's remarkable book, I had no idea about the profound impact it would have on me. Brielle, at the tender age of 10, bravely shares her journey of living with alopecia, a condition that affects not just her physical appearance, but also her emotional well-being.

We are given an intimate glimpse into a mother's unwavering love and support as she witnesses her daughter navigate the challenges of losing her hair and adjusting to a new sense of normalcy. The raw honesty and vulnerability displayed in these pages brought me to tears, as I empathized with the struggles both Jenise and Brielle faced. Through their story, I gained invaluable insights into the complexities of parenting a child with alopecia, as well as the resilience that can emerge from adversity.

This book is not just a story; it is a beacon of hope for anyone touched by alopecia, whether directly or indirectly. It serves as a powerful reminder of the importance of compassion, acceptance, and embracing one's uniqueness. Jenise and Brielle's experiences will undoubtedly leave a lasting impression on readers of all ages.

I wholeheartedly recommend this book to anyone seeking inspiration, enlightenment, or simply a heartwarming tale of love and resilience. It is a testament to the power of storytelling to educate, uplift, and unite us all.

Felicia Flores
Creator/ Founder of Baldie Con

It was at Baldie Con, a vibrant gathering of bald women showcasing their strength, resilience, and beauty, that I first met Brielle Belay. Even in a room filled with inspiring individuals, there was something magnetic about her. I started rocking my bald head at 40 after being diagnosed with a form of alopecia, while Brielle began her journey before she was 10. Founding the first Black-owned clean beauty brand to launch on Ulta and HSN, I felt losing my hair was a loss of my identification with beauty. Like Brielle, being a model, actress, and influencer, hair loss wasn't part of the original glam look. But Brielle embraced a higher calling—self-acceptance.

In a world where beauty standards confine us within narrow definitions, the journey toward self-acceptance and empowerment becomes a profound act of defiance and courage. It is with immense pleasure and admiration that I write this foreword for Brielle Belay's remarkable book on alopecia—a work that sheds light on the complexities of living with this condition and offers hope and inspiration for countless individuals.

What sets this book apart is Brielle's unwavering commitment to fostering a sense of community and empowerment. She emphasizes that alopecia does not define one's worth or potential. Through her words, she builds a bridge of understanding and compassion, encouraging readers to embrace their unique beauty and support one another in their journeys.

As you turn the pages of this book, you will be moved by stories of resilience and triumph. You will find yourself reflecting on the true meaning of beauty and the power of embracing our authentic selves. Brielle Belay has created a work that is not only informative but transformative. It is a call to action for greater awareness, empathy, and acceptance.

To everyone who picks up this book, know that you are not alone. Whether you are personally affected by alopecia or seeking to understand and support someone who is, this book is a gift. It is a testament to the human spirit, a celebration of the beauty that lies within us all, and motivation to rock our crowns!

Thank you, Brielle, for your courage, wisdom, and unwavering dedication to this important cause. Your words will undoubtedly change lives and inspire a new generation to see beauty through a more compassionate and inclusive lens.

With deepest respect and admiration,

Kim Roxie
Founder of Lamik Beauty

Table of Contents

Part I: Introductions... 1

    Introductions to Our Memoir............................... 2

    Introduction to Us.. 6

Part II: Before Alopecia.. 10

    Brielle's Early Years... 11

    Life As We Knew it... 19

Part III: Our Alopecia Journey................................... 23

    And So, Alopecia Began...................................... 24

    The Treatments.. 33

    About Alopecia... 39

    Challenging Experiences......................................45

Part IV: Overcoming Challenges & Acceptance................53

    Free at Last..54

    Coping Strategies & Support.............................. 58

Part V: Empowerment & Triumph.............................72

    The Show Must Go On.......................................73

Part VI: Conclusion.. 77

    The Bond is Bonding 78

    Closing Remarks to the Reader...........................80

    Acknowledgments 84

    Epilogue by April Showers..................................87

Part I:
Introductions

Introductions to Our Memoir

Jenise:

In the face of adversity, my daughter Brielle and I went on a transformative journey through her experience with alopecia. This memoir is our shared story, a testament to the strength of an eight-year-old girl who rose above the difficulties she faced and emerged as a source of inspiration. This memoir is also a testament to a mother who learned a new meaning of beauty by rejecting society's views and embracing beauty from God's perspective. As a mother, I navigated a range of emotions and obstacles with her, personally witnessing my daughter's incredible resilience.

Our narrative unfolds together, with threads of courage, vulnerability, and an unbreakable bond between a mother and her beautiful daughter. I cannot hide the fact that I grappled with fear, desperate to shield my daughter and make everything right. Yet, this story unapologetically reveals the truth: there are challenges we can't fix. Our touching story explores a mother's vulnerability and the idea of allowing God to lead you through the most trying circumstances. Our story demonstrates the fundamental lesson that hardships can lead to amazing outcomes. And don't get it twisted, this book is about something more than alopecia; it is about accepting anything that makes you question your worth, value, or beauty.

We want you to understand that true beauty is beyond physical features, and imperfections do not define us. We hope to inspire people all over the world with Brielle's and my experiences. We want every reader to find comfort in acceptance, realizing that clarity and security in one's true self can dissolve insecurities. This is a story of triumph, an invitation to embrace the beauty within, and a message that resonates with every soul navigating the complexities of self-acceptance.

Brielle:

You know how sometimes things can happen that make you sad or scared? Well, that happened to me when my hair started to fall out because of alopecia. I no longer have hair like most people do, and it's an ongoing challenge for me. I can't lie and say I don't miss my hair. I loved my hair, and not having it makes me feel a bit different. But in a short period of time, I realized something really important – it's okay to be different!

In our memoir, I'll share all the moments when alopecia made me feel a bit sad. But guess what, though? I also talk about all the times I felt super strong and happy too!

Alopecia led me on some interesting adventures, and I can't wait to take you along on my journey. We even put pictures in our memoir because seeing what we went through will help you connect to us and our story.

Most of all, I want you to know that no matter what you look like on the outside, you're beautiful. We all are! Even when things are tough, we can find good stuff and be happy. I'm writing this because I want you to feel inspired and really believe that you're awesome just the way you are. I hope my story helps you see that true beauty is all about what's inside our hearts.

5

Introduction to Us

Jenise:

If you're like me, you want to know a little something about the individual who is sharing information with you. So, before we begin our story, Brielle and I will briefly introduce ourselves.

My name is Jenise Belay. I was born and raised in Saint Louis, Missouri. I am the daughter of Clifton and Katie and the youngest of three children. Growing up, I was an outgoing girl. Entertainment runs through my blood, as I grew up in a musically inclined home. I pursued careers as a professional singer and model. I am a mother, an entrepreneur, and a momager.

When I'm not busy submitting auditions for the girls, practicing for pageants, and handling all my mommy duties, I try to squeeze in some time for myself. I enjoy finding a nice restaurant or relaxing at a resort. I've always enjoyed spending time by the water, fishing, and appreciating the blessings of nature from God. That is me in a nutshell.

Brielle:

My name is Brielle Belay. I was born and raised in Atlanta, GA. I am the daughter of Jenise Belay and Daniel Belay. I have an older sister named Brooklyn; she's my best friend, and I do everything with her. I also have a big brother named Nasir; he's super tall and annoying, and he thinks he's so cool. But he's the best brother ever.

I recently turned 10 and just had the ultimate 10th glow-up party; it was the best. I love building Legos and fixing things. One day, I want to be an architect. I aspire to become the first female to design the world's largest building. I love playing Roblox with my sister and classmates, as well as cuddling with my two dogs, Brodie and Bella. I enjoy cooking with my mom and hanging out with friends.

School is something I love, and my favorite subject is math. I can solve any math problem in no time; I think I'm a math whiz. Right now, I love reading Greek mythology books; it's so cool. I also enjoy watching Stranger Things with my sister; it's my favorite series.

About me

Part II:
Before Alopecia

Brielle's Early Years

Jenise:

To describe Brielle's early years, let me start by saying that she was such a beautiful baby. My goodness! She came out just…. perfect. When she was born, she had these big, bluish-gray eyes, long lashes, and a head full of hair. She was gorgeous, to say the least. One of my fondest memories of her as a baby is when my dad started calling her his Pretty Bird. He would say she was the prettiest bird in the world.

As for her personality, Brielle was outgoing, loud, and wild. She had, and still has, such a big personality, which is honestly a reflection of her big sister. Brielle often looked up to her sister and always wanted to do everything she did. Therefore, it goes without saying that I had two outgoing, loud, and wild Pretty Birds.

Like her big sister, Brielle always loved to sing and dance. Modeling and prancing were the ways she made her way around the house. She always wanted to be seen, and let me say this: it wasn't hard for her to get the attention of others.

Jenise continued:

One thing that stood out to me was that wherever we went, people would always stop us to say how gorgeous Brielle was. They marveled at her beautiful eyes and her gorgeous hair. Brielle always had this presence about her that had the power to literally make people stop in their tracks to compliment her.

I can't deny that it would sometimes get overwhelming, for lack of better words, when people would just stop and talk to me about Brielle. If I had to put my finger on it, it was something inside of me that felt like the attention could create a sense of pressure or heightened expectation on my baby. It was kind of like she lived in a space where her beauty was something that she always heard about, which I understood because she was simply beautiful.

Due to the frequent compliments, I decided to get my daughters into modeling. This led Brielle to land her first modeling job at the age of 6 weeks. As she grew older, she participated in pageants and print modeling. She worked with many top brands for print and commercials. When she competed in pageants, she would often win. She had the ability to captivate an audience with her beauty, and over the years, both my girls became pageant queens. The first pageant I ever entered them in was called 'Little Miss So

Chic,' and they fell in love with it; the rest is history. From there, we started participating in local pageants that turned into national pageants and even some international ones.

Brielle had a presence and confidence that couldn't be taught; it was just natural. It was as if she and her sister were born to be stars. What we loved most about pageantry was the fact that it wasn't just about beauty but also poise. It taught valuable life lessons, such as building friendships and giving back to the community. They learned important skills like interviewing, carrying themselves with grace, networking, and working a room. I'm proud to say that my girls are equipped for anything, and I believe the exposure to pageantry played a significant role.

Brielle:

Growing up, I would say I used to terrorize the house. I always looked up to my sister. If she did something, I would do the same thing, but I always wanted to do it better. We often competed, even over whose hair was the longest. What can I say? I always enjoyed competing.

I remember going places, and people would come up to compliment my sister and me. They'd say, "Oh, you're so pretty." I would just smile and say thank you. Receiving compliments was normal for me, and it made me feel pretty and important.

Growing up, I always played with Legos; building things was my favorite activity, and it still is. If you gave me some Legos, I would spend hours in the room trying to build everything in one day. My mom would often have to make me take a break. That's how much I love building.

Brielle continued:

As I was growing up, I started modeling, singing, and acting. I began modeling as a newborn, and I started singing by the time I could talk. When we were babies, my mom would always sing to us, making up nursery rhyme songs, and we would sing along. To me, my mom is the best singer in the whole wide world, and I wanted to sing just like her. We often sang together in the car. We love singing songs by Aretha Franklin and Beyonce. She's also my favorite. As we got older, my mom really developed us and taught us everything about music and entertainment since she used to be in the business. It was always fun working with her; it was quality time for me.

I've been doing beauty pageants since the age of four. My first pageant was 'Little Miss So Chic.' Since that pageant, I have won several others. What I enjoy about pageants is the sisterhood and getting to meet new friends. I also love to do the volunteer work that comes with being a part of pageants, as well as the prize packages. Most of the time, the prizes include free trips.

Life As We Knew it

Jenise:

Brielle and I have always shared a strong bond, and she's undoubtedly a mama's girl—just like her sister. When the girls were growing up, I started a YouTube channel for them, featuring our own cooking shows where they would use their Easy Bake Oven. We even had a catchy intro: "Hi, I'm Brooklyn, Hi, I'm Brielle, and we are the Belay sisters." It was incredibly cute, and we always found joy in these little activities together. Our shared love for food persists, with Brielle and her sister Brooke still enjoying cooking, especially during the holidays. It's a tradition that brings us even closer.

Brielle:

I always loved cooking with my mom. We whip up all kinds of dishes together—mashed potatoes, green beans, chicken, mac and cheese, you name it— all that good stuff. We watch movies and play together. Oh, and I even do her makeup, and I'm pretty good at it. I enjoy braiding her hair because I know a little something about hair. Honestly, I could go on and on about all the things we do together because it's a lot, and I'm so grateful to share these moments with my mom. My mom and I have this cool bond through things like food, hair, and singing. It might sound weird because my hair went away from alopecia, but hair still brings us closer together. Losing it somehow made our bond super strong. It was already strong because of love, but it's something about facing a challenge together.

Jenise:

Speaking of bonding through hair, I really took pride in both of my daughters' hair. When they turned about two and three years old, their hair just grew like magic. I was very thankful that they both had very healthy heads of hair. Like I mentioned, we would do YouTube videos, and oftentimes I would record myself doing their hair and showing the products that I was using. I would monitor and share how much it would grow over time.

As Brielle mentioned, she and her sister would oftentimes compete: who had the longest hair? It was just hilarious, especially since they were so young. They valued their hair, and it was something that, you know, as girls, we took pride in. Growing up, I was taught that hair is your glory and your crown. I cannot deny that it is something I instilled in my girls. Hair plays a major role in our lives. We had special moments bonding through it. Nothing on this earth can break our bond, so losing her hair didn't impact that. But the alopecia broke our bond with hair.

Part III:
Our Alopecia Journey

And So, Alopecia Began

Jenise:

I was the first person to discover Brielle's bald spot. I remember it so vividly; a few days prior, I noticed her hair was shedding like crazy. However, I figured it was because we had just left a pageant. She had been wearing her hair in a ponytail for over a week, and I thought it may have been from the heat of styling her hair over and over. I remember telling her, "Wow, Brielle, I'm going to need to deep condition your hair; it's shedding like crazy."

A few days passed, and I decided to go ahead and wash her hair that evening. I did my usual routine, laying her on the kitchen counter and fluffing out her hair to wet it. As I removed the ponytail holder and began fluffing her hair, I saw a big bald spot right in the middle of her head. In that moment, it was like I was having an out-of-body experience, feeling numb and discombobulated. I started shaking uncontrollably, thinking, 'OMG! Jesus.'

Brielle looked up at me and said, "What, Mom?" I quickly ran into the next room, pacing back and forth, trying to digest what I had just witnessed. I felt like I wanted to throw up, and my body felt like it was on fire. I was sweating and couldn't think straight. How was I going to tell her that she had a bald spot the size of a golf ball?

I remember trying to recap what had happened with her hair over the weekend. It's crazy because Brielle's hair was the best it had looked in a long time at the pageant, and I remember telling her that. It was so healthy, thick, and luscious. I think she even won best hair. After I recapped, I immediately went into blame mode. I called her father and said, "I'm going to kill her!" He asked who, and I said the hair stylist. I was shaking and so angry, saying she burned my baby and tried to hide it. He told me to calm down and tell him what was wrong, but I couldn't get it out; I was crying so much. Shortly after, probably just a three-minute time difference, but it felt like forever, Brielle came to the door screaming, "Mom, my hair!"

At that moment, all I could do was hold her and let her cry. I said, "Don't worry, Mommy's going to fix it." She said, "Mom, they are going to bully me." At that moment, all I could think about was how I was going to fix this and quickly.

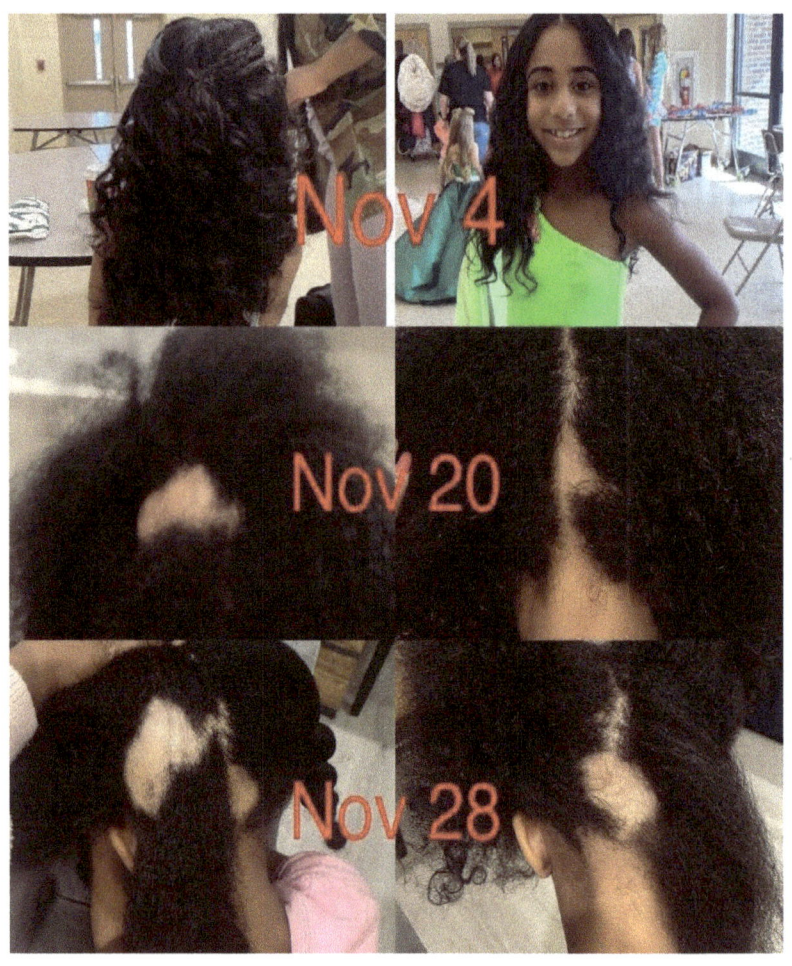

So, I took her back to the kitchen and started washing her hair to see what I missed. As I combed through her hair, clumps of hair were just falling out. It was like it was melting off her scalp. I had never seen anything like it. Looking back, I remember her sister was even crying; hair was our thing, and we were truly emotionally attached to it.

After washing her hair, I discovered a few more spots, so I did my best to hide them in ponytails. Then, we went upstairs and laid together, and I just told her everything would be fine. I watched her fall asleep and prayed over her, asking God to heal her body.

After I left her room, I contacted the stylist, of course, to blame her. To this day, I feel terrible because I needed someone to blame, and she was the only person I let in Brielle's hair, so of course, she was an easy target. It was like I was going through the same emotions as a death: blame, anger, confusion, helplessness, fear, sadness. I remember staying up all night, googling, and trying to find a solution. The next morning, I called my dermatologist and told her I needed her to see Brielle right away; it was an emergency, and they allowed us to come in that day.

When we got in, she asked us what happened and what we had done leading up to that moment. When she saw the spot, she smiled and said, "Aww, Mom, this is fixable; it looks like heat damage mixed with a little alopecia." She then looked at me and said, "We can treat this slowly or aggressively." Since I'm a fixer, of course, I wanted aggressive and fast. But I didn't know the aggressive treatment would cause so much pain to my child that I regret to this day. This was the beginning of our nightmare. She gave Brielle over 20 steroid injections in her scalp, and Brielle screamed bloody murder. Shortly after that visit, we thought we had a solution, but that was only the beginning. Days later, more hair started falling out; it just wouldn't stop. It was melting off so fast that there was nothing I could do to stop it. And so, the journey began.

Brielle:

I felt so confused. I remember my mommy looking in shock and running off. At first, she didn't say much. I started feeling around my head, and the skin was smooth. I remember my sister coming over to me, putting her hand over her mouth, and saying, "Brielle, you don't have any hair." She then ran upstairs, and I jumped off the counter, running to my mom. She had locked herself in a room and was talking to someone, and I remember screaming. She opened the door when I started screaming and crying. I was so scared. I really didn't know what happened to me, but I knew it must be bad. I was crying, "Mommy, my hair, what's wrong?" I had butterflies in my stomach. I cried so hard I wanted to throw up, and I remember saying, "Mommy, people will bully me." My mom hugged me tightly. We were both scared, but she kept telling me, "Baby, mommy is going to fix it; don't worry." I believed her because my mom always makes things better. She said, "Brielle, you have a bald spot in the back of your head. Did the stylist burn you?" And I told her, "No, Mom." She kept asking, "Are you sure? Does it burn?" And I said, "Mom, no…" but I really wasn't sure.

My mom got off the floor and took me back into the kitchen to wash my hair and examine it. I cried the entire time. Watching my mom cry as she washed my hair was a first. This was usually a time when we would bond, and she would tell me how beautiful I was and ask me about school and what I did for the day.

That time, it felt like someone had died. It all felt like a bad nightmare, and I wanted it to stop. After washing my hair, she took me to the couch to style it. I could see her hand shaking as she styled my hair. After she finished, she told me that everything was going to be alright and how beautiful I was. Then she came upstairs and held me until I fell asleep.

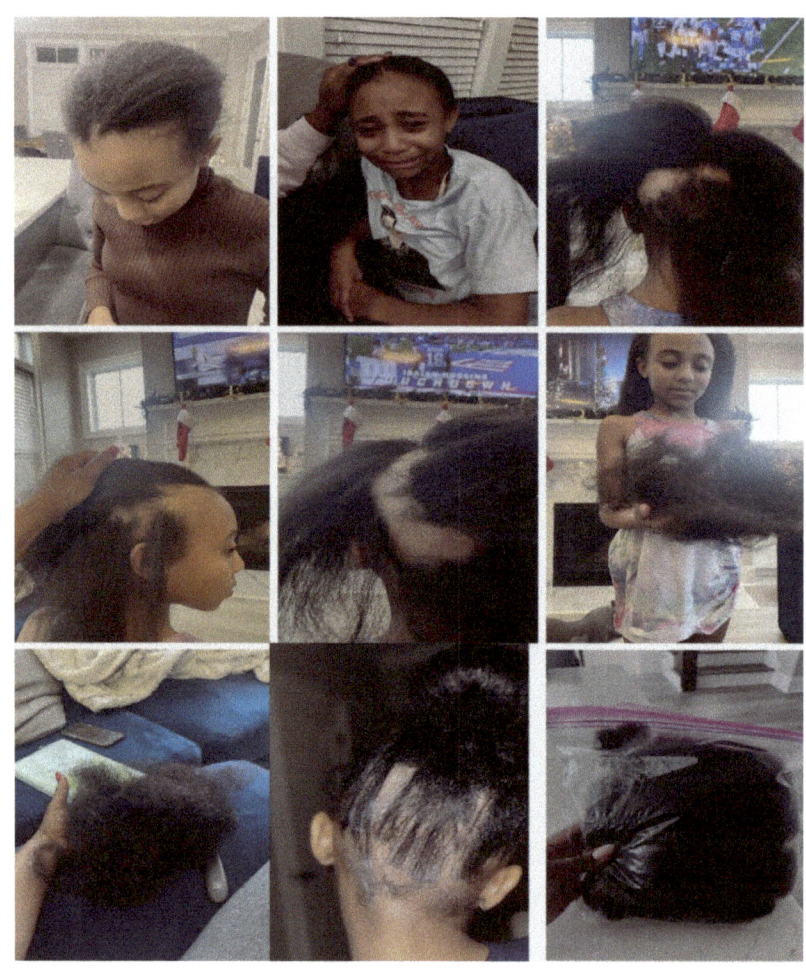

Jenise:

As the alopecia progressed, we navigated our way through several different specialists. We received different answers, no answers, and even encountered combativeness. I grew angrier with each visit as we continued to face uncertainty and resistance from the specialists. I developed insomnia because I was obsessed, unable to stop thinking about what was happening to her. I've always been known as a fixer, and I just needed to fix this. I had to get the answer.

There were even questions and theories from physicians suggesting that the COVID vaccination could have played a role in the onset of her alopecia. Prior to this happening, we had done the vaccination booster shot to be in compliance with the entertainment industry because the COVID vaccination was a requirement for Brielle to work. About a week after she received her booster shot, I started to notice her getting sick. She had a lingering cough and runny nose that wouldn't go away for weeks. I had so many thoughts and theories swirling in my mind. I had so many fears and ruminated on unanswerable questions like: What are people going to say? Will kids make fun of her? Why? Why is this happening to her?

Once one of the doctors said that it was alopecia, I did so much research on what alopecia was and how it affects people. I mean, I literally spent hours and days trying to understand how and if I could fix it.

Brielle:

We went to so many doctors. I want to say it was about 10 of them. Most of them couldn't really tell us what was happening, which I didn't understand because they were doctors. Something was definitely happening because I went from having a head full of hair to having so many bald spots.

I remember when one of the doctors told us that it may be a little heat damage mixed with alopecia. I panicked because alopecia didn't sound good. I don't remember the doctor explaining what alopecia was; I just knew it sounded terrifying. And I was right. I tried all types of creams, and I got some injections. It was so terrible that I screamed the entire time. That experience motivated me to learn more about alopecia because I didn't want to have to go through pain again. I needed to know how often I would need injections and if my hair would grow back. I had so many questions.

The Treatments

Jenise:

We went to a dermatologist, and Brielle's condition seemed to be downplayed—a story I plan to dive into further in the 'Challenging Experiences' section of this book. Feeling dismissed, I reached out to her pediatrician for guidance and support. It was important to me to ensure there weren't any underlying internal issues. I wanted to rule out every possibility, from lupus and cancer to stress and more. It was clear to me that this was not right and that there had to be something triggering it. I was committed to finding the cause and the cure.

So, I started researching what could cause hair loss, and most sources pointed to things like thyroid imbalances, vitamin D deficiency, hormonal issues, and more. I wanted every test to rule everything out. I remember feeling frustrated when her pediatrician didn't want to do a whole panel of tests. I insisted, saying, "Why not? I'm willing to pay for it, and I don't care about the cost." But she didn't think all the tests were necessary, which was nerve-wracking because I felt like no one was taking the urgency of the situation seriously enough.

I sought second- and third-party opinions, looking for the best doctors I could find. I was racing against time to save her hair and treat whatever was making her sick. Within two weeks, I took Brielle to see an allergist, an endocrinologist, two other dermatologists, a trichologist, and a gastroenterologist. I was determined to get to the bottom of it.

When the blood test results came in, they found that Brielle had a stomach infection, low vitamin D, and elevated hormones. This led to a long journey of treatments. The trichologist treated Brielle holistically, using techniques such as microneedling, UV light therapy, vitamin supplementation, and scalp massage. The gastroenterologist performed a procedure where they put Brielle to sleep to insert a camera into her stomach and see what was happening. Once we found the infection, we started treating it with medicine.

I realized I needed to change Brielle's diet, so we cut out sugar and processed foods and started juicing. Cutting out sugar was tough for Brielle because she loved candy and sweets, but I found out that sugar can make hair loss worse.

Finally, the endocrinologist treated Brielle's hormone imbalance with injections. Brielle went through a lot during this time; there were tears shed during some of the procedures, from both of us. She was poked, prodded, and x-rayed for weeks. I was in full-on 'I gotta fix this' mode. It was exhausting for both of us—I missed work, and she missed a lot of school.

In the end, we couldn't save her hair, but we did uncover an underlying medical condition we didn't know she had. The biggest lesson I learned from this experience is to always get blood work done on my kids during every physical. Usually, during a physical, they usually only ask questions and measure height and weight. Unless it's something major, they're not checking for anything they can't see with their eyes.

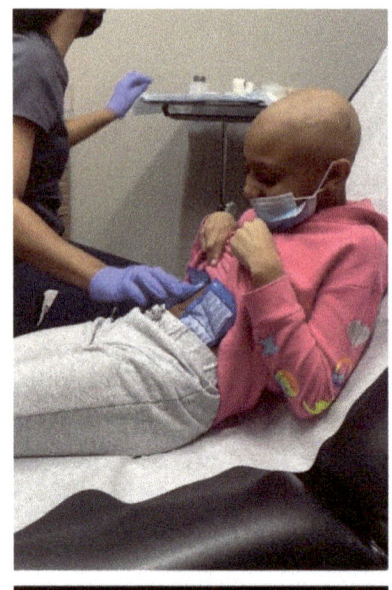

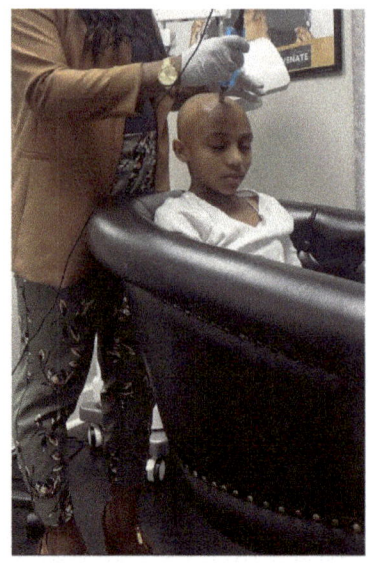

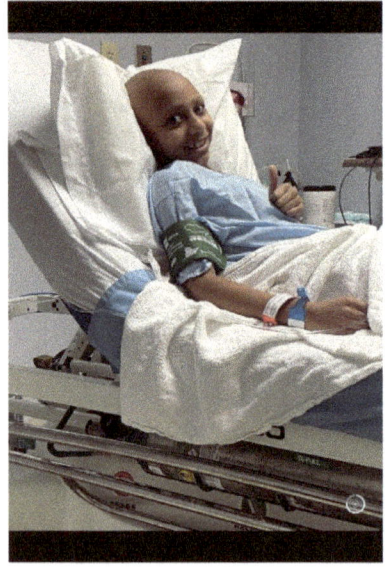

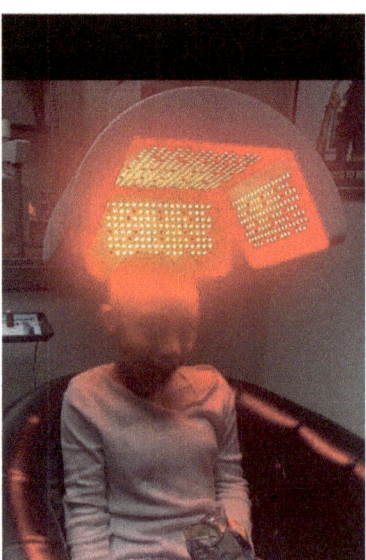

Brielle:

After I found out my hair was falling out, we went to the dermatologist so I could receive injections in my head, which were the worst shots I've ever had. It felt like being stung by 100 wasps, and I'm really afraid of them. I had over 20 injections because I kept moving. Afterward, my scalp hurt so bad that it was painful to touch. The next time I got injections, I just couldn't take it. It hurt so badly that I ran out of the room; I refused to let them do any more. I wanted to get better, but I wasn't willing to go through the pain of the shots.

I remember the doctor first telling us it was alopecia areata, but over time, it turned out to be Universalis. We never really knew how severe my alopecia was until my hair stopped growing altogether. After we tried the injections, I remember getting a lot of blood work done and plenty of testing.

When I got the results back and decided I couldn't handle the scalp injections, my dermatologist told us about Dupixent, which were injections but not in the head. They were supposed to help grow my hair back, but it didn't really work. I got these injections every month in my stomach, so I got used to it.

Another treatment I tried was with a trichologist, a person who helps with hair loss and gives natural treatments. She was one of the doctors who looked at my hormones and found they were really elevated. I had a lot of things going on with my body, and it was really bad. She did my first treatment, and I'm not going to lie, the scalp massage felt really good.

Later on, we continued to go to different doctors about my hormones until we could find a cure. The thing is, we never really knew what caused the alopecia. Could it have been caused by the COVID vaccine, or maybe my hormones? We don't know. All we knew was that it came out of nowhere. For months, I kept getting injections, going to the doctor, trying treatments, and it was really overwhelming for me and my mom. But we both wanted to fix the problem, and I wanted my hair back.

About Alopecia

Jenise:

As I mentioned earlier, I've done a ton of research on alopecia. I also made sure Brielle was educated on what was going on with her. Therefore, we can provide an informed overview of alopecia. However, we recommend that you conduct further research on your own since there are many forms of alopecia. The most common type is alopecia areata, an autoimmune condition where the immune system mistakenly attacks hair follicles, resulting in hair loss.

Brielle:

There are many different types of alopecia. The most common one, as my mom mentioned, is alopecia areata. Then there is alopecia totalis. Just as it sounds, your entire scalp experiences hair loss. Another type is alopecia universalis, where the immune system attacks hair follicles not only on the scalp but also on the body, including eyebrows and eyelashes, which is what I have. The list goes on. Alopecia can come at any age, from when you're just a little kid, like 2 years old, to adulthood. Alopecia can basically show up whenever it chooses.

Jenise:

One of the most unsettling discoveries I made in my research was the tragic case of a young girl who took her own life due to bullying related to her alopecia. Alopecia itself might not cause physical pain, but the emotional and mental toll it has on individuals is significant. When combined with the cruelty of bullying, it becomes a recipe for disaster. My heartfelt condolences go out to the family of that beautiful girl. It's truly heartbreaking.

One major frustration I encountered on this journey is the way health insurance views alopecia treatment—not as a medical necessity, but as cosmetic procedures. It baffles me because, in reality, one's mental and emotional health is at stake. There have been instances of people tragically ending their lives due to the emotional turmoil of having alopecia, underscoring the severity of the condition. Despite some progress in treatments and increased empathy, there is still a lack of understanding about the effects of alopecia, which can be life-altering for many.

For most people, their hair, eyebrows, and eyelashes play a crucial role in shaping their face and enhancing features. Losing these can feel like losing a part of one's identity, altering their appearance, and, at times, making them appear unwell. The impact on self-esteem is significant, affecting millions psychologically. Alopecia is unkind because it strikes unexpectedly—some experience slow hair loss, while others wake up to find balls of hair on their pillows. This unpredictability makes it an emotionally traumatizing experience. For Brielle, it happened rapidly—from a photoshoot with a head full of long, beautiful hair to the next month, a photoshoot with a fully bald head. The speed of change added to Brielle's trauma.

Before Alopecia

One Month After Alopecia

Challenging Experiences

Brielle:

The biggest initial challenge that I faced after my hair loss was that I didn't like looking at myself in the mirror. I looked at myself in the mirror, but I never actually thought anything of myself. If I had to look in the mirror, I definitely avoided looking at my head; I just focused on my clothes. The reason I avoided the mirror was because I did not recognize myself, especially after losing my eyebrows and lashes. I felt like I looked like a totally different kid. I thought I was ugly. Having no hair at all made me so sad. To me, I looked like a boy. I didn't even want to go out in public and show my head.

Jenise:

The initial challenge I faced was feeling unheard. I felt that nobody was listening or helping the way we needed to be helped. As noted earlier, we had been to several doctors and all types of specialists. A lot of times, I was denied real answers. It was mind-boggling to be told that her hair loss was normal and that it would grow back. It was more frustrating to be told that Brielle was fine. There is nothing normal or fine about an 8-year-old losing her hair. If it was so normal, then why was it news to me?!

So, I specifically found this one dermatologist who was a black lady, thinking that she would understand the importance of a black woman, or, I should say, a black girl, losing her hair. I wanted Brielle to see the African American dermatologist because I just knew that someone who identified with us would understand how serious this issue was. I took all of Brielle's hair that she lost and stored it in a large bag to ask the dermatologist to test the hair follicles.

She called me crazy and told me that there's nothing wrong and that Brielle would be fine. I remember yelling and screaming at this lady, "You don't know what you're talking about. How dare you tell me that I'm crazy? Just test the hair!" Well, she pretty much kicked me out. I felt hopeless and defeated, and I was PISSED. It was very challenging to not be heard by doctors. Unfortunately, African Americans are the most unheard race when it comes to anything medical; it's not a secret.

Brielle:

When I went out in public, people would just look at me. I shouldn't say they looked at me because they would STARE, and it made me very uncomfortable. So, I thought that, in the beginning, it would be better to hide my head. I started to wear turbans. I had hundreds of turbans that I would wear out. I had a wig too, but I never actually wore the wig besides one time.

I was often called a boy by a lot of people who didn't know me. It was different for me to experience people thinking I was a boy. It made me sad and I hated when people called me the wrong gender.

Going back to school was even harder because people would make fun of me. I was called names that I didn't really like. I was called things like Baldy and Mr. Clean, which I found very offensive. Like really?! It made me upset that people could be so cruel and say mean stuff like that. I must admit that it got to me a couple of times. Some kids thought I had cancer because I looked ill. The thought of people thinking I had cancer did not feel good.

Brielle continued:

When I first returned, no one in my class really understood anything about alopecia. Kids would ask me questions or make statements about my hair like, "What happened? You had long hair, and now it's just all gone!"

It took a lot for me just to walk into the halls because kindergarteners would point and stare. I would say that about a week into the semester, I started to feel less confident, and that's not the person I am. I'm a confident person. I'm an energetic person who loves to talk to everyone. So, I surprised myself when I couldn't be confident, and I didn't want to talk to others. I started to feel insecure about myself. I started thinking that I was not enough. I cried to my mom that I didn't want to go back to school because of the bullying, staring, and questions.

Jenise:

Another big challenge I faced was feeling like a failure as her mom. I didn't know how to handle the situation. I was ashamed. I was scared for her. I did everything to nurture my baby's self-esteem, and I saw it being chipped away with every piece of hair that was falling. I was angry. I was disappointed. I felt like I failed her because I couldn't stop the hair from falling out. Simply put, I just felt useless.

Brielle:

Another challenging experience I've had since losing my hair is that I haven't booked a lot of acting jobs because most of the time they want to get someone with long hair or at least some hair. So, it's challenging for me because in the beginning, it was not like that. I had a lot of hair and would easily book gigs, but now that has slowed down. It hasn't stopped me completely, but I haven't been getting as many jobs lately.

I've also been receiving fewer compliments. Some people compliment me on my looks, but it's not as often as it used to be. They'll say, "Oh, you're so pretty being bald." With that 'being bald' statement, it doesn't make it feel the same as before. A lot of people used to compliment my eyes, and I don't hear that anymore. I don't have my eyebrows or my eyelashes, so that has changed my appearance a lot and has obviously changed how people compliment me.

Jenise:

Society, for the most part, hasn't fully embraced the concept of baldness, which creates a challenge within itself. As of the time of this memoir, in the past couple of years, there has been the most discussion about alopecia in history, largely due to advocates such as Jada Pinkett, who publicly shared that she has alopecia areata. We genuinely appreciate everyone's advocacy for people with alopecia.

For many years, baldness has been considered taboo, something people kept hidden from public view. But now, with the advocacy of alopecia, we are starting to see more and more people come out and own their truth. They are coming from behind the wigs and really expressing how free and liberating they feel now that they are accepting their baldness.

Hollywood and the entertainment industry are still catching up, and acceptance is slowly emerging. Beauty expectations are often perpetuated through media, advertising, and social media, influencing people to conform to a particular ideal. This can create pressure and impact self-esteem. That is why it's important to challenge and redefine beauty norms. I am determined to make sure that Brielle's self-worth is not stripped away by comparing herself to societal norms and standards.

On the whole, Brielle has admirably navigated the shift where people might not give her as much attention as she's accustomed to. What brings me joy is witnessing her confidence, which has redeveloped since declining after becoming bald. The support and encouragement from those around her have played a crucial role, contributing to her ability to overcome the challenge of losing her hair and her newfound confidence, which seems to radiate enough for ten people. It's truly amazing to witness this transformation as she steps into this new phase of her life.

Part IV:
Overcoming Challenges & Acceptance

Free at Last

Brielle:

The very first time I decided I was done hiding my head was when I was on a trip to Saint Louis, and we went to a bouncy house. I snatched off my turban inside the bouncy house place because my head was so hot from sweating. I remember being scared to think about what people were thinking about me. A lot of people were looking at me, which made me uncomfortable.

At the same time, I was feeling free. I just had to take it off and overcome worrying about what everyone was thinking. Another time, I decided to wear a wig to a football game. For some reason, I felt uncomfortable in it. So, I decided to just be myself and show who I truly was without the wig. I could not take it any longer, so I snatched the wig off in the car. I just yanked it right off. It was so funny and so freeing. I was touching my head. I was like, "Oh, this is soft. I love my head!" I felt like this is who I am, and I think I should go on without hiding.

Jenise:

When I spazzed out on the doctor who dismissed me as crazy, I vividly remember Brielle's calming words, "Mom, Mom, stop. I'm okay. Mom." At that moment, a shift occurred within me. I realized it wasn't only my burden anymore. It was time for me to let Brielle carry this, and all I could do was hold her hand and guide her through this challenging journey. As her mother, the fear of letting go was huge—allowing her to face rejection, stares, questions, laughter, and bullying. Despite my strong desire to shield her from difficult experiences, I knew I had to release my grip.

It was like a sense of peace had come over me. I said, "God, I know you're going to take care of her. You're going to cover my child. You're going to cover YOUR child." It freed me when Brielle, with her big, pretty eyes, looked up and declared, "Mom, I'm okay. I'm ready. I'm ready to face the world." It provided a piece of hope during a dark mental state. It got so dark for me because I felt like the enemy was attacking my daughter, my family, and her health. I just didn't understand. I thought I did everything right, and the experience left me in doubt about that.

Losing her hair felt like a form of death, as if we were grieving the loss of something we once celebrated. I had taught them to take pride in their hair, as it was glorious, bringing happiness and joy. So, losing it took some of our joy away. However, at that appointment, my emotional journey shifted from grief and anger to a blend of frustration and hope. My primary role became supporting Brielle. As her mom, I had to be her biggest advocate, ready to fight for her and provide undying support.

The first thing I really had to fight for was the best medical treatment. After being brushed off, as if her hair falling out was no big deal, I had to firmly assert the need for comprehensive blood work to ensure her overall health. It was a crucial step before fully accepting that alopecia was the culprit. I'm thankful we dove deeper because it uncovered various issues—gut problems, elevated hormones, and a vitamin D deficiency, as we mentioned in the treatment section. All these elements were attacking Brielle's body at once, contributing significantly to her hair loss, or, we'll say, exacerbating her hair loss. Knowing all of those things puts us in a stronger position to address those problems and see if correcting them would have any impact.

Coping Strategies & Support

Jenise:

I wasn't going to allow anybody to break her down. When Brielle first cut her hair off, it was during the holidays, and I had really worked hard to build her self-esteem and get her to a comfortable place of acceptance. However, I started to notice that a week into school, she began to regress, and I couldn't understand why. Eventually, she told me that people were starting to bully her and stare at her, and she didn't want to go to school anymore, as she mentioned earlier.

So, I went up to the school to talk to the staff and told them that Brielle didn't want to go to school anymore because she was being bullied. I had to tell them that I'm trying to do everything in my power to keep her uplifted and groom her to keep loving herself through all the changes, so the bullying needed to stop. At first, I felt brushed off and ignored, so I showed them an article about the young girl with alopecia who had taken her own life because of bullying. I was not going to allow the school to fail my child. I was not going to sit there and build my child up at home, telling her how beautiful she was, only to allow her to go to school and be told otherwise.

I explained to them that Brielle is supposed to be protected at school and that she goes to school to learn and to be in a safe space, but some of the kids were tearing her down. So, I asked if I could create an initiative to educate the other kids because kids can be cruel, both intentionally and unintentionally. My goal was to protect Brielle, first and foremost, and also to teach the kids at her school that they need to respect people who are different.

One thing I can appreciate is that the school listened to me. I think they realized this was a bigger issue than they originally thought, and I'm forever grateful that they did. So, later that week, they did a segment on alopecia and explained to the kids through the intercom and on video what alopecia was. At one point, Brielle got an opportunity to speak with her classmates about her experience with alopecia. She was able to explain what it was, and the kids were able to ask questions.

I'm really thankful to her teacher, Miss Ellis, because she was a huge advocate for Brielle and supported her all year. Honestly, I think she was sent by God. She was a new teacher who came from a different state and was still learning about her students and the school. But she just adored Brielle from day one. I mean, she was truly a hero in my eyes because she was my eyes and ears when I wasn't there to protect Brielle. That really helped Brielle thrive in school, and her grades never slipped. Miss Ellis played a major role in that, and I am just forever grateful to her.

Brielle:

It made me happy that the bullying stopped. Thanks to my mom, the school played a video about alopecia, and I was able to talk about it in order to educate the kids at my school. The young kids, like the kindergarteners, still stare, but I do not let it bother me because they are young and they don't really know what is going on. But overall, I'm just happy to see that everything is better now because I didn't want to stop going to school because I like school. On my report card that semester, I got all A's and one B because I was able to focus on what the teacher was teaching instead of worrying what my classmates thought about me.

Miss Ellis was like my bodyguard; she protected me from everything. I think I was her favorite. I was even able to eat lunch with her every Friday. She made me feel safe. She helped bring back my confidence as a student and helped me stay focused. She will forever be my favorite teacher and friend. I love you, Miss Ellis.

Brielle continued:

When I first started losing my hair, I hid my head in turbans so the kids at school didn't see my hair loss, which is why I didn't experience bullying right away. During my holiday break, I was ready to shave the rest of my hair off because it was so hard to see the big bald spots all over my head. I was nervous because I loved my hair, but at the same time, it was not the same, and I was ready to start over.

We got on a Zoom call with my family members so they could support me during my big chop. I remember watching my hair fall to the ground in big balls. At that point, I started crying. It was like I had all these mixed emotions of joy and sadness at the same time.

Jenise:

I've always been a mom who took pride in my children, and I consistently shared their accomplishments on social media. That wasn't going to change. So, I allowed people to join us on this journey. We did a Facebook Live, sharing updates on what was happening with Brielle, and we recorded a video of when we cut off her hair so that people could walk through this journey with her, and she knew she wasn't alone. I remember when we decided to cut her hair, I wanted it to be a moment that she would never forget.

I hired a female barber and a wig specialist to customize a wig for Brielle, and we turned it into a celebration. We popped confetti, had balloons, and had roses for her. I wanted her to feel loved, and as scary as it was, I think she knew she had people in her corner. I organized a Zoom call with my family and played every encouraging song that Brielle loved. I wanted her to know that this wouldn't define her, that she was still beautiful, and that we were going to get through this. I wanted her to understand that this was just a moment in her life, and she was still destined for greatness.

I remember that moment being sacred. As the barber shaved off the rest of Brielle's hair, Brielle's face lit up. She started glowing, and it was like she just had this peace come over her that was so welcoming. She was just so beautiful bald. I could see her face even more, and it was just so beautiful to see. I made sure to remind her daily that she was beautiful. I wanted my empowerment to fuel her own self-empowerment, so I also put affirmations on her mirror so she could remind herself how beautiful, strong, and brave she is because she truly is all of those things. She was very brave, and I am incredibly proud of her.

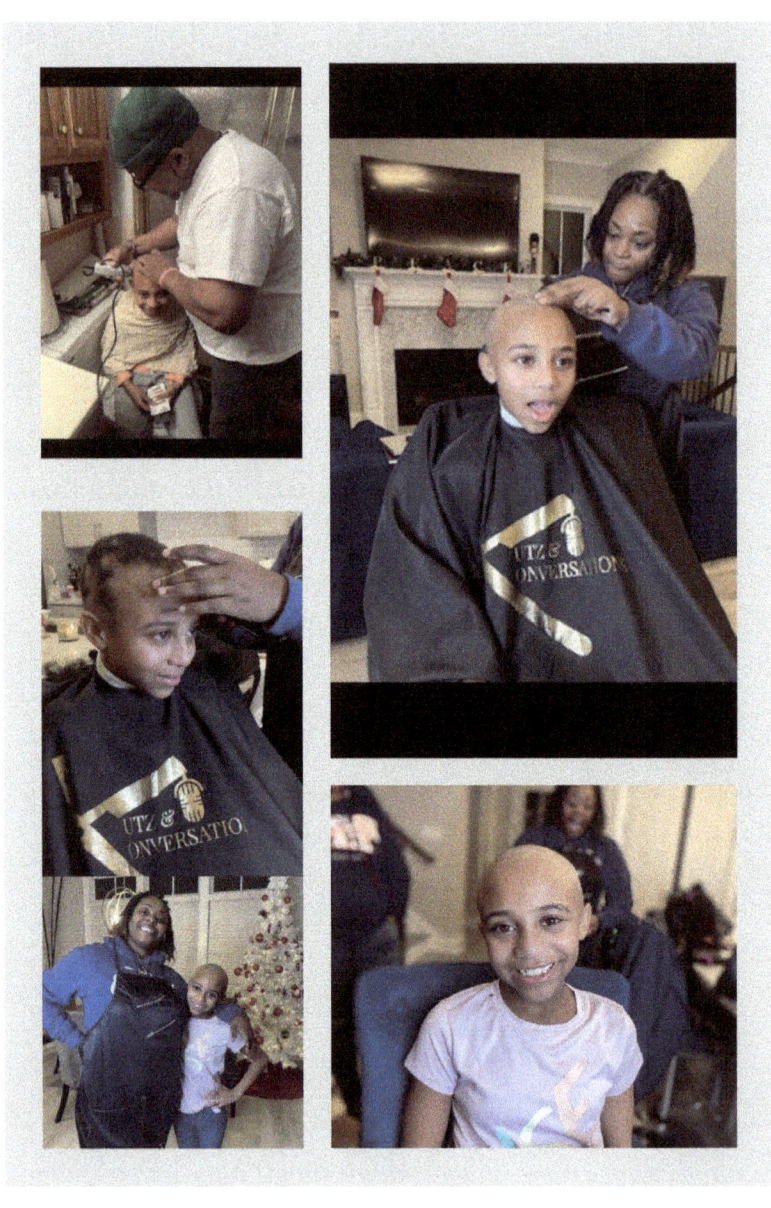

Brielle:

Now that I have really embraced my beauty, I never wear wigs, and if I choose to wear a turban, it's because I want to, not because I feel like I have to. I believe I look good with or without hair. I've always thought I was beautiful, and now my confidence has grown even stronger. Sometimes, I still have moments of insecurity, especially when I see other girls with long hair, but it doesn't affect me as much as it did before. I really like myself, and I don't mind standing out.

Since losing my hair, I started researching famous people who are bald, and I found out there are a lot out there, including many who were going through some of the same experiences as me around the same time. They were all starting to step out from behind their wigs and be their true selves.

Because I'm into modeling and acting, I admire the model Jeana Turner and even the actor from Stranger Things who played Eleven, Milly Bobby. Seeing them has given me the power to keep moving forward. Knowing that so many people are going through what I'm going through has made me feel less alone, and that's where I draw my strength from. Also, I must mention that my sister has been a huge support;

that girl will jump at anyone who messes with me. Let's just say I got people.

Jenise:

As I was seeking answers, I initiated contact with advocates and sought therapy groups to connect Brielle with individuals facing similar challenges. One organization that became a crucial part of our journey was CAP Kids, the Children Alopecia Project—a supportive community for kids dealing with alopecia. It's a beautiful space where children can see others like them and openly discuss their shared struggles.

A classmate of mine, Dalen, had dealt with alopecia as a child, and I noticed he was a spokesperson for the organization. He connected me with the founder and provided resources to kick-start our village. Additionally, I reached out to a beloved Soror and friend, Nasha, who also experienced alopecia. As a model and actor, she displayed remarkable resilience throughout her hair loss journey. Observing her strength over the years, I wanted her to be a supportive presence in our journey as well.

Jenise continued:

Another thing I did to help Brielle cope and gain support was to connect her with two other little girls who were around the same age. One of the little girls was actually experiencing hair loss at the same time. This connection was God-sent as her mom and I started to support each other and figure out ways to uplift our daughters during this challenging time.

Our experience with alopecia brought many different people into our lives. After sharing on Facebook, hundreds of people reached out, offering support and advice on treating her condition, each playing a big role in our collective healing. One key person was Felicia Flores, an advocate for alopecia, who founded the organization Baldie Con.

Brielle:

One day, my mom was at a restaurant, and she saw a pretty lady. My mom went up to Miss Flores and said, "Hi, I'm sorry to bother you, but I wanted to ask, do you have alopecia?" Miss Flores replied, "Oh yeah, I do." So, my mom said, "Ohh, my daughter has alopecia too." My mom asked if Miss Flores could offer advice or help. That's when we were introduced to a therapist named Miss Nikhol, who also has alopecia.

With Miss Nikhol, we had sessions where we talked about how I felt about alopecia and talked about my experience in the beginning. We went through my entire journey with alopecia, basically.

Miss Felicia also introduced us to Baldie Con, and she asked me and my mom to speak at the event. When we arrived, everyone was so nice; I felt so special. I was blown away because I've never seen so many bald, beautiful women in my life. Before, I probably only saw one or two. So, I was happy to see people that I could relate to.

We got up on the stage and talked about our journey and how hard it was to find doctors. The women there were saying, "You're very brave; I really look up to you." They were telling me that I was really pretty and complimented me on my confidence. Many of the women shared with me that they struggled in the beginning too and didn't have the confidence that I have at my age.

I felt like a celebrity being around people like me. They all wanted to take pictures with me and asked to stay in contact, adding me on social media. I took so many pictures that day. I also had a chance to speak with the lady from Vogue magazine. And guess what? She gave me a book called "Sparkle," about a black girl who looks just like me and who's bald.

Jenise:

It was crazy that Brielle looked just like the picture of the girl in the book. The author reached out and was impressed by Brielle as well. Brielle made a significant impact on so many people at Baldie Con—hundreds of women who were bald and struggling, without an outlet or support. To see a young 9-year-old be so confident was inspiring to them. Many approached us, expressing how Brielle had changed their lives and how her story had inspired them. It was a really impactful platform for Brielle.

From there, people started to see the videos that we posted, and she started going viral. People reached out to tell Brielle how much of an inspiration she was and how they had been hiding behind their wigs, caps, and scarves for years, lacking the courage to step out bald and free like she did.

Through this platform, we shared our story and used our voices, finding it therapeutic and healing. It contributed to Brielle's newfound sense of purpose and to mine as well. My role was not just to support her but to demonstrate that, despite the challenges, the show must go on. Brielle is still beautiful, and she can continue pursuing all the dreams she had before alopecia entered our lives.

Part V:

Empowerment & Triumph

The Show Must Go On

Jenise:

"You are still going to do pageants. You're still going to model. You are still going to act. Your hair does not define you," were my exact words to Brielle before I encouraged her to continue participating in pageants. About a month after she completely lost her hair, I entered her in a pageant because I wanted her to understand that losing her hair didn't mean she couldn't pursue the things she loved. She participated in that pageant, and she won. Winning took her to the nationals, and it was a huge confidence booster for her. It boosted her confidence immensely.

Brielle:

I decided to participate in another pageant to prove that I'm still the same person, just without hair, and that it doesn't change anything about me. During this pageant, I felt really confident in myself. People were saying I was so brave, and I was happy that I decided to take part. I ended up winning the Southern States title in this pageant, which was really, really, really cool.

Brielle continued:

I went to the nationals after that, and although I didn't win, I made such an impact on Mrs. Neely, who is the director of 'Ideal Miss'. She created an award in my honor, and it's now a national platform for the pageant! I was so shocked and honored! I find that to be so cool! The award is about being impactful, brave, and strong. I just can't believe that actually happened. An award named after me? Wow. Okay!

Jenise:

Brielle has always had a positive outlook, and to see her soar after such a tough time is refreshing. Recently, she booked a part where she played a main character for Afro Unicorn's live-action TV show. She's also been pursuing her passion for music. Despite losing her hair, I always believed that the show must go on! We're still going to thrive in school and in the entertainment business. We just have to pivot, break down barriers, and demonstrate to the world that bald is also beautiful! I can genuinely say that Brielle has navigated and shifted her perspective on this journey. She has taken control of her life in a positive way and refused to let alopecia define her.

Part VI: Conclusion

The Bond is Bonding

Jenise:

I would say that our mother-daughter journey throughout this experience has undeniably strengthened our bond, opening my eyes to a profound understanding of true beauty. It's not about the external, like your hair, right? True beauty comes from within—it's a divine gift from God. This journey was a wake-up call for me, challenging the notion I had instilled in my daughters that beauty was tied to their hair and other external factors. Facing alopecia was a transformative experience that prompted us to redefine and embrace beauty as God intended it to be. Brielle and I now share a mutual understanding that true beauty lies within, as external appearances can be deceiving; you can possess the looks on the outside and be ugly on the inside.

Brielle:

That is so true. People can be so pretty, but can be so mean at the same time, and at that point their beauty doesn't matter. Who you are on the inside matters the most. Like, what's your personality?

Jenise and Brielle:

How do you treat people?!

Jenise:

How you treat people is the biggest key to beauty! This experience with Brielle has impacted me because it has revealed the importance of seeing beyond the surface. We often get entangled in vanity, not taking the time to genuinely know someone for who they are. Stripping away the fancy clothes and hair forces you to look at a person and understand what resides in their heart, revealing their true essence. This journey has been a significant source of personal growth for me—as a mom, a daughter, and a friend. It taught me to accept people, to cultivate compassion and empathy, and to love unconditionally.

Brielle:

I'm so grateful to my mom. She has been there for me every step of the way, during the hardest and the best moments. She is my superhero, and she always pushed me to stay confident, even when people were making fun of me. The struggle was hard, but she never let me give up. She mentored me, and I'm blessed to have her as my mom.

Closing Remarks to The Reader

Brielle:

I want to tell you that you are enough, and don't let anyone say otherwise. Being yourself is perfect—I hope you know that. As Afro Unicorn always says, you're unique, magical, and divine. Also, if you see someone who looks a bit different, see them as unique and perfect too. And if you catch anyone being mean to someone just because they're different, speak up for them. That's what being a good person is all about!

Jenise:

I want to encourage mothers to support their child the way he or she wants to be supported. Whatever they may go through, they have their own story to tell. It's their life. Our role is to stand with them, offering unwavering support. The instinct to fix things and make their challenges our own is strong, but it's through these experiences that we foster resilience and raise amazing kids. Even in the face of trauma, there's a journey they must navigate. Our responsibility is to love them and keep them motivated to fight. Let's show them they are worth every ounce of the fight!

Jenise continued:

I strongly recommend incorporating prayer into your journey with your children. If you have faith in God and find yourself facing challenging moments, hold onto that belief. I've witnessed God's incredible ability to transform tragedy into triumph and pain into purpose. It's something I truly believe in, as what was once pain, frustration, and hurt has evolved into a beautiful, inspiring story.

We hope our story inspires you to embrace your uniqueness without shame. Don't hide, whether it's due to a lack of hair or any other challenge; remember, you are perfect just the way you are. Even in the midst of life-altering circumstances, you will prevail, and the journey will build incredible character. Our aspiration is that our story touches and inspires you, just as the stories of others have impacted us. Thank you for being a part of this journey!

Acknowledgements

Brielle:

As I reflect on my journey, I just want to give a big thanks to my family. They've been super supportive, and I love them for that. Thanks to my third-grade teacher, Miss Ellis. She's been there for me the whole school year, standing up for me when no one else would. You rock, Miss Ellis!

And to all my friends, you guys are like my second family. Thanks for being there for me. Shout-out to my sister too; when someone's being mean, you're always there to stand up for me. I love you!

Mom, you're the real MVP. You've been running around, talking to everyone, and making sure I'm okay. Thanks for everything you do. Dad, thank you for all the love and support you have given to me throughout my journey with alopecia, and you still support me even now when I feel down; you always have a way to get me back up again. And to everyone reading my story, thank you too! Your positive vibes mean a lot to me. Send some good energy my way for the rest of my journey. You're awesome!

Jenise:

Reflecting on this journey fills me with immense gratitude. I want to express my thanks to God for instilling the strength within me to walk this path alongside Brielle. Watching her transformation from a little baby to a young lady, a warrior, and a fighter is truly remarkable. Brielle embodies bravery and resilience in a way that goes beyond my own understanding.

Witnessing her emerge beautifully from this experience, especially considering the challenges others have faced, fills my heart with gratitude. While she had her moments of tears and feeling down, she never lingered there. Brielle always wore a smile and demonstrated bravery. I am sincerely thankful for the positive spirit God has placed within her, guiding her through this challenging journey.

I also want to extend my gratitude to Brielle's third-grade teacher, Miss Ellis. She served as the ears, eyes, and shield over my child during school hours, which are the toughest times. To our family and friends who supported me in coping with this journey, helping me accept the imperfections that turned out to be beautifully imperfect, I am thankful. This experience has shifted my perspective, making me realize what beauty truly is. I wouldn't change a thing because it has given me the strength to view life differently.

At a time when life seemed to attack our family on multiple fronts, God knew where this journey would lead us. It has opened doors to better opportunities, introduced us to incredible people, and allowed us to savor life as God intended. For all of this, I am grateful.

Epilogue by April Showers

As the founder and CEO of Afro Unicorn, I am deeply honored to reflect on 'Still Rocking My Crown: A Memoir of a Mother & Daughter's Experience with Alopecia' by Brielle and Jenise Belay.

I first connected with Brielle five years ago, when she and her sister, Brooklyn, became our very first models for Afro Unicorn. I vividly remember them proudly sporting Afro Unicorn shirts in front of their home. Brielle's vibrant personality always stood out in every photo and video. Although I didn't meet Brielle in person until two years ago, the connection was immediate, especially considering her longstanding involvement with my brand since its inception.

Afro Unicorn stands for celebrating diversity and empowering women and children of color. As the first black woman to own a fully licensed character brand in major retail, I take pride in our mission. Like Brielle, my entrepreneurial journey started young, with me founding my first business at the age of nineteen and eventually opening my own State Farm office. My ability to navigate multiple successful businesses while being a dedicated single mother earned me the nickname "unicorn" from a friend. Brielle embodies the essence of our brand, embracing her uniqueness and resilience in the face of challenges like alopecia.

Today, Afro Unicorn has blossomed into a global phenomenon, with products gracing the shelves of major retailers like Walmart, Target, and Amazon. Despite our remarkable growth, we remain grounded in our grassroots origins, prioritizing authentic representation. Brielle, along with several Afro Unicorn kid ambassadors, will feature in our live-action series, which debuted at the 10th anniversary of the Bentonville Film Festival.

As a mother, multi-business owner, author, and speaker, my passion lies in imparting my entrepreneurial spirit to the next generation, which is what the live-action series is about. I also aim to promote self-love and empowerment. I believe that Brielle is a perfect spokesperson because she has demonstrated both qualities, and I believe that she will bring out those qualities in others.

Moreover, through the Afro Unicorn Foundation, we strive to inspire individuals worldwide to embrace their uniqueness and make a positive impact on the world. Brielle's journey, resilience, and courage exemplify the core values of Afro Unicorn, reinforcing our commitment to diversity, empowerment, and authenticity. Together, we continue to rock our crowns proudly, illuminating the path for generations to come!

www.ingramcontent.com/pod-product-compliance
Lightning Source LLC
Chambersburg PA
CBHW051226120626
46547CB00013B/1522